AF418424

Yas Press
University of New Hampshire
English Department
230 Hamilton Smith Hall
Durham, NH 03824

Managing Editor: Danielle Jones
Poetry Editor: M.P. Carver

Cover art © Julee Holcombe

Cover and interior designer: Andrew Griswold
Managing Editor: Molly McGrath
Published in partnership with Pink Eraser Press

YAS POETRY SERIES

An Anthology of Poems by USNH Students

Volume 3 | 2026

CONTENTS

Introduction

Congratulations to all of the New Hampshire undergraduate and graduate-level poets whose work is included in this year's anthology. At UNH, we often have students in introductory poetry classes read this anthology along with other classic and contemporary poets, so in addition to congratulations, let me say something even more important: thank you.

Thank you for knowing that the world needs poetry today. It needs new ways of looking at old problems when the old rehearsed and received stances and assumptions no longer seem to work. It needs your feeling, your humor, your wit, and your sense of adventure. It needs the synthesis of metaphor and simile. It needs the compressed meaning that images convey, but only when they are run through the unique miracle of the individual who lives and feels and remembers things in jumbled ways. Virginia Wolf says that the world never asks for poems, but this anthology shows that the world needs your poetry, just as the world needs more free people of consciousness and compassion and its unlikely twin, humor, needs their fresh eyes, needs their open ears, their impulse to build, to make from a spirit of play, alertness, and discipline.

We also need poetry because poetry helps us remember. The techniques and arcana of poetry, rhythm, rhyme, even the pauses, the caesuras, the punctuation, and the withheld punctuation are all in the service of the entertainment of memory. When we remember a poem, we remember to feel, to live with our senses. We remember the rawness of feeling and the relief and pleasure of play. And the voices of poets, being companionable, being good company, remind us we are not alone. These are all reasons for gratitude. Once again, thank you, poets and readers. And all readers of poems become poets when they read. Thank you.

David Blair, M.F.A.
Lecturer of Poetry
Department of English, MFA Writing Program
The University of New Hampshire

THE WILDCATS POETRY
PRIZE-WINNERS

———————

Interview

(After José Olivarez)

Blake Harrsch

Where is your home?

In the pink bedroom walls
I could never paint over.
Mom said there was no point
investing in a house we might lose.

I peeled the eviction notice off the door
as the school bus rounded the corner,
walked toward the driveway's end.

Where is your home?

My first apartment. Smack in the center
of the queen bed and me, sprawled out
like a starfish flaunting its pink.

The landlord said if I want to put things
on the wall: No nails. Command Strips only.
And certainly, no paint.

Where is your home?

A week ago, I would have said his arms.

He used to say he lived with his aunt
and a batch of cousins. A favor
until he finished school.

He used to say I couldn't come over
because they already hated
this country enough. Couldn't bear
to see him loving white skin, too.

Really, the blankets of his queen
bed were already taken, wrapped
around the swollen belly of his pregnant wife.

Where is your home?

In the citrine ring from Marshall's.
Feeling fancy when I asked to see it
outside of the display case.

In the parking lot, when I peeled
the red sticker off and slipped it on.

In Grandmother's hospital bed,
when she rubbed and rubbed it, spent
her last breaths exalting its beauty before asking
if insurance ever cut the check for my totaled car.

—

Where is your home?

Half in the cobblestone streets
of Rome. Violinist playing,
just like the movies. I was Hilary Duff.

Half in Jersey, buried in my parents' hearts.

All of me in the in-between:
the WhatsApp call to avoid
another Verizon charge.
(I racked up fees the day before.
First time out of the country).

I peeled myself from the cloud
of Chianti Classico, picked up.

Mom makes sure I know she can't pay
for the phone bill and that I need to send
photos. She passes the phone to Dad.

He tells me he's jealous. If he could study
abroad, he'd book a one-way, ditch
the books on arrival and never come home.

Where is your home?

Between the lines congratulating me
on my acceptance. When I get there.

When I bloom alongside the packs
budding from our pockets, as we stand
outside the bar, talking to strangers
no newer to us than we are to one another.

Where is your home?

The gravel driveway, becoming whole
as snow falls into the cracks.

In the attic. In the box with the Christmas tree
we can't put up because my parents got a cat
in the in-between. I brought my homework
for winter break: the paint cans in my trunk,
full of marshmallow gloss, swirling.

Giving Back

Emory Stevens

I've been trying to be the better person that
my mother tells me to be when we're on the phone. So
I baked some cookies and took them to Bronstein Park.
It was a hot one. The weather app said 85 but feels like 91.
This girl, Christina, was layered up in thick coats
and wool blankets. Someone leaned her against the lamppost and
made all of us feel better about the situation.
I brought her two cookies and shook her shoulder gently. "What?"
she rasped out. A cigarette was dying between her fingertips.
I tried to look at her, but I kept looking at it instead. "Hi, I'm
     Emory and—"
"What's that?" "Oh, sorry," then a little louder, "Hi! I'm Emory
and—"
"No." "No?" "No—what is that?" she said. The cigarette flicked
     slightly over
to the dollar store paper plate I carried. "Oh, these? These are
     cookies"
I said, "Vanilla chai." Christina said nothing and so then I said
     nothing.
She was bent drastically over herself in a way that made me
     uncomfortable.
I shielded my eyes from the sun with my hand. I was beginning to
sweat. This isn't how things were supposed to go. She was

supposed to take something from me. I brushed off the fine line
of ants that had started crawling up her unmoving arm.
Another organizer came over to take charge as I was clearly
    floundering.
"We're gonna move you to the shade, okay, Christina?"
She said with confidence. Probably worried about heat
stroke, I thought. We put our hands on her waist and she cried out,
    "No!"
"No?" "I'm too cold inside, I need the sunlight." The organizer
    made a face
and wandered back to the group. She had given it the good ol'
    college try.
I felt trapped, but also in complete control. She was safe, for now. I
put her dead cigarette in one of her coat pockets. She was cold to
    the touch.
I was burning up. Meanwhile, the ants had taken crumbs of
her cookies to procure a mighty feast. I got up to be where I
wanted to be. Christina was already there.

The Earth Was Leaking Again

Ariana Cooney

It started sometime after midnight—
a slow gurgle beneath the rhododendrons.
By morning, the Earth was leaking again.

"I told you this would happen," said Lydia,
standing in her galoshes,
holding a teacup under a dripping oak.
"It's not groundwater. It's memory."

I knelt down and touched the mud.
It was warm, like soup left too long on the stove.
A worm wriggled past my finger,
muttering something about lost treaties
and overdue apologies.

"All these years," Lydia said,
"and we never even asked if it needed a break.
We just assumed it liked being round
and silent and trodden on."

From the garden, a daffodil screamed.
It was a sharp, elegant scream,
like a violin string snapping in a cathedral.

Then the wind showed up,
dragging a plastic chair and wearing sunglasses.
"Don't look at me," it said.
"I just move things around."

The trees began to tilt, just slightly,
like they were considering a mutiny.

"I think we should apologize," I said.
"To whom?" Lydia asked.
"To all of it. The rocks, the insects,
even the algae. Especially the algae."

We wrote a letter on the back of a seed packet
and buried it beneath the compost bin.
Lydia lit a candle and placed it on the dirt.

For a moment, everything went very still.
Even the leaking stopped.

Then the Earth sighed—
a long, tired sound like a door closing slowly—
and swallowed the candle whole.

We could be animals—floating forever

Hazel J. Hall

When will we stop pacifying ourselves
     like we don't exist because of love,   because of paintings,
          because of brushstrokes and
               breaststrokes through clear water?
          I keep trying to pretend there isn't oil
             in this water, in
                  our paintings, inside of
            my soul; no,   it's not that my heart has died—
         it's just gotten quieter recently. You know,
I'm just scared we are turning back into animals
     (if we ever stopped being animals).   I know
          we're responsible for our choices but
     I don't know how we got here. How
          chatbots write our emails for us like
              we are better pacified   like pop love songs
                are enough to distill the oil in our water
         like AI is a pacifist and our planet
            can be reconciled in pixelated paintings.
Could I ever do enough
to convince myself I'm not   just some animal?
         What will I do to reconcile
            the forests we have ravaged
               to create this

machine learning? This deep learning like
cogs and wires have ever gotten so deep into learning   like
this was all something we so desperately needed
like if the first guy didn't do it
someone else would have been forced to do it
in his place like
we need innovation more than we need the sun at dawn and
water on the horizon line.
I'm pacifying myself   like one breaststroke
will keep me floating forever. Hold on,   let me ask ChatGPT
about forever. Let me see if it can be as animalistic
as me.   Let me gaze upon
the forests that grow inside this
non-consensual culmination of us and
our information and our ideas and
our paintings.
Let me ask ChatGPT if it believes it is pacified.
If it knows how closely linked it is
to animals or if it does not claim
its heritage   like I do not pretend to be some
pacified animal like
I do not wonder if ChatGPT
is the difference between me
and animals
like we ever stopped being animals.

THE UNIVERSITY SYSTEM OF NEW HAMPSHIRE STUDENT POEMS

I Want to Talk of Big Things

C.E. Victor

The street is dark
Lamps glow like dead stars
and my blood is a black hole
that I cannot run from

Dawn brings the song of the sun
and we match notes as I try to get lost
Feet make marks in the ground
My path to the lake is clear

I call you and we talk
of dads and kings and God with a big G
And I ask if we are bound for hell
and you say we are just bound for dirt

Each day I see the lake and think I will drown in it

If the Soil Spoke/Pulse for a Profit

LW

When we were crafted to fear eyes that caught brief reflections
We were created from cartilage and dust
Evolution has saved us a spot at God's table as great apes
In fairness, we do not rise above other animals
Morals and our morality organized us into single filed lines
We may be apex only in name, claws replaced for an acrylic substitute
    layered with gems
Our long black and brown hairs for warmth replaced for silkworm
    farmed suits
Our canines slowly straightening out with metals and whitening
    with chemicals
Our bones won't remember the plastic, oils and gases
The child that finds your fossils won't know about your cubicle or
    grades
The bugs and fungi will slowly eat at your flesh, regardless.

Mama

Clay Phelps

Mama why don't you like me
Can you tell me what to do
Mama aren't you supposed to
Love your only daughter too?

Mama why don't you like me
Can you tell me what to do
Cuz I was only put on this earth
To try to do right by you

And my mother was a critique
Her mother before her too
I'm my own worst enemy
And the same goes for you

Mama why don't you like me?
Can you tell me what to do
Dad, he says you love me
But we both know that's not true

And mama will you miss me
When everything fades to blue
Mama do you forgive me
Like I forgave you?

Mr. Unexpected

Kathryn Campbell

I had seen you only once before,
I honestly didn't think anything of it.
I knew I might run into you again,
Just not like this.
Never did the thought cross my mind that the crowd around us
     wouldn't matter,
That the voices around us froze when I looked at you.

We can talk about everything or nothing at all.
The day I met you we did just that.
We talked about cars, and shoes, and music

I don't know why I'm starting to feel this way.
I never asked for this,
Nor did I ever try to search for it.
But here you are,
Talking to me about anything that comes to mind,
Turning the silence into something I want to share.

I promised myself to be alone for a while,
And while that thought hasn't left my mind,
You haven't either.
You are Mr. Unexpected.

Corks? Cursed.

Samantha Christen

Corks of different sizes, layered in dust.
Labels vague, beautiful and full of potential.
Peeling from the edges of their homes like aged wallpaper.
Bottles in various shapes, containing different potions.
Liquors, wines, sugary concoctions meant to blend.
Whites, pinks, oranges, blues. An occasional red gifted from
    strangers
Or those far from my thoughts, who know nothing about my taste.
Bent Straws, shiny glasses, worn coasters all rest, ready to be called
    upon,
Like alternates on the bench,
Breathless with anticipation
Of being chosen.

A glass holds the lucky elixir of choice
To fix today's doubts.
A hand swirls, tips and swivels the tall stem,
Balancing the world's remedy in its head.
All of the world's mistakes also take up residence here.
Every wrong word said, every awkward silence, every time your
    doubt was right.

—

One sip cascades delicately past the expectant lips
To the desperate tongue, feigning for attention, approval, resolve.

The elixir works quick. Like a curse that cracks the brain like a
    shattered windshield
And leaves the pieces behind, askew.
A long, sharp nail of Pino Grigio moves pleasurably slow through
    the ridges of my pale brain.
Feels so severe as the two hemispheres split
And yet it relieves me of any more decisions today.
One last sip washes over my worn tastebuds.
Rest now, tomorrow's bottle awaits.

Put out to pasture

Liam Raphael Gleason

I believe in nothing so great as the night shift
when I once watched two boys
cajole three silver-skirted girls into their car
they must have been off to burn their hay
    when I ran
    it was said that racing
    was burning the hay in the barn

Another time in a house
on the fruitless edges of an apple orchard
working the night shift and shuffling my feet
swaying my hips to my own chosen music
    I fashioned a sword of empty beer cans
    and called myself a king

I locked a young woman out of the house
on the concrete steps she sat
watching the thin end of the day roll by
I spoke to her through the door
about back pockets
    and what men put in them

This past November's Halloween
I approached a sweet
Red-lipped king's guard
and let her know
that I had seen her before
and would again
        she snapped her heels shut
        and gave me a salute

told me all about The Gay Science
how she owes her life
to Harpo Marx and Johnny Cash
so I told her all about returns to form
and Exile on Main Street
        how all the corn and silos in the fall made
        someone say back home could be Kansas

Capture My Beauty in the Photobox

Keyshaun Sullivan

There rose wings shimmering faintly, pinned in their stillness as though a breeze once passed through and never quite lifted, each vein holding in pale threads of blue and silver that flickered, with one lilt of light wilting the glass in hums with the roped mutter, banded wing to another with the quiet hush of a meadow in one larger blushed-white space pinned down in a box, the glass tilted inwards, glass bending where no grass stood. And the guilt of now motion-flushed air was in something unshushed, a breathless waiting, a pause prolonged, the faintest rustle, unrushed, and lingered in absence as if the room itself remembered the quickness of flight, the trembling of fields at dusk, the fragile murmur of days that will not return, and yet the wings spread, cast their color like the ghost of a motion, tender, unresolved, a melancholy that quivered against the silence without release.

Snapped together to be complete

and snapped forever.

iPhone Parents

Naomi Deann Planchet

I see the glowing light
That flickers on her face;
She is trapped and captive
Miles and states and countries
Far, far—away.

I crawl a little closer
To the corner of her eyes,
And there I try to draw
Her back to the world, to life—
To me.

I laugh and play and jump
And dance—feeling something
Change; I look, yet see her eyes
Still stuck—beyond reality,
I stop.

I stare, I cry, I yell
It's not fair—
This is not fair!
She stops and moves her eyes,

A glimmer of hope, then a flicker of light
Glows before me—still.

My Mother, Me

Carrie Alice Hiltz

"I like what you're doing," my mother says, as I comb
the knots from her hair. "It feels very loving. Are you going to
    braid it?"

She's been losing teeth rapidly these past few years.
She won't brush them, won't

take care of herself,
and they're rotting in her gums.

As I brush her hair, I think about the last time
she visited—how I picked her up from the shelter.

She tricked me, told me she needed to go to the hospital,
was having suicidal thoughts.

But when she got in my car, she was feeling better.
She wanted to go home with me.

While we sat in my living room, and I tried to figure out
what to do with her, my son fell backwards off the couch

and split his head wide open.

When he started to scream, I thought he was just being dramatic.
I got up slowly to check on him.

When I saw all the blood, I screamed too.

In the emergency room I held a cloth to his head.
He waited so stoically. All the nurses thought he was so brave,

but when the doctor came with her staple gun,
four nurses had to hold him down,

and all I could do was hold his hand and listen
to him cry to me for help.

Harlot

Anna Mangum

noun

1. (derogatory, dated) a woman who has many casual sexual
encounters or relationships

lips untouched like the tops of the magnolia trees with their long
    fragrant flowers
tickling the sweet-smelling southern air, those very lips were the lips
    I shut tight
as I drove to his house after school, the thin lips I didn't know what
    to do with, always
moving my mouth like an echo to his call, I did not show my
    stomach to him, I did not
show myself, my lips opened in a thank you as he handed me a book
    in his living room,
the lips of his wife were there, the seventh month of her pregnancy
    was there, the daughter
and the son already born were there, the mother-in-law was there,
    and I stood with my face
to my own face in a mirror, my blue eye looking at my blue eye, it
    hurt to see who I was, I
wanted to go home to the freshly-mowed grass and inhale, I wanted
    to know my mother held me

in the palm of her hand and made me her world, love turning into
    itself, love leaving the body to
create another body, a body that goes to places alone, the body now
    a girl lacking flight and
feathers and pluck, I watched myself in the mirror and saw a girl
    standing in her teacher's living
room, wishing for kudzu to swallow her whole, its invasiveness
    spreading, eating its likeness,
even though her lips were untouched, her body was still a secret, I
    tried coming home to myself
but the mother-in-law stared at me like she could read my attraction
    and blamed me for his.

2. (archaic) a prostitute

Proverbs 2:16
Do not let your heart turn aside to her ways,
Do not stray into her paths

Melatonin

Amaiyah Olavarria

I spend most my days tucked away,
enveloped in the dust and darkness.
How easy it is to forget, day by day,
hour by hour, minute by minute.
The seconds that pass unrelenting.
Skin painted earl grey, now a ghost.
Because forgetting doesn't mean he's gone.
Sweat-slicked forehead, startled awake.
Because sometimes I wake up,
I wake up four inches shorter,
weaker. I wake up terrified, angry,
and angrier. I wake up ruined, again,
and again, and again. Don't wake up.
The memory replaying, despite all that
effort. To live, to breathe, to forget.
Because sometimes I wake up,
right back in that house,
all over again.

his dialectic.

Kendall Elizabeth

your fire
burns me cold
you shatter me whole
the way you wind me up and unravel my soul
kills me until i'm alive again
because there is no life like the death of you
and i hate it
i hate the way i love you
and love the way i hate you
desires i don't want but own
i possess the truth and crave lies
like *"i don't love you"*
because it would be so much easier
to fall out of this abyss that threatens to kiss
my emptiness
until she's full

Dah

Ivan Byrde

today is a somber day
where she sits in the passenger side
of my brain
her hands clasped together,
rings made from melted spoons,
twisted around her fingers.

lavender and chamomile,
refreshing chemical cucumber smells.
mint growing outside
in the abandoned garden.
her shaky hands
pushing a cigarette to her mouth,
eyes fixed upward
at the burn pile.

I used to worry the cigarette would set her hair on fire
with how much spray was holding it up.
and whenever I get a whiff
of Winstons,
I instinctively turn my head.
sometimes turning up and to the side
like I'm about to tug on a shirt

and ask to go to the library.
it was always a yes.

listening to Mr. Tambourine Man
and speaking what I remember
of the old tongue;
just to carry with me
the knowledge
that we are one
in the same,
with the same predispositions.
just a different time,
where I was raised by her daughter.
I got to see myself become freer.

I started taking meds again
because my hands started to anxiously shake.
part of me hesitated,
because I knew the shaking was because

I'm like you.

petrARchan Sonnet (POachEd arTIstiCAlly)

Liz Blanchette

With eyes akin to bloodshot moon of night,
She wields her pen of pathos like a gun.
To crumpled corners should the stanzas run,
She'll lure them deftly back into the light.
The thrill of hunting rhymes just out of sight;
A bounty much too promising to shun.
She's careful not to maim a word for fun,
For poems are naught but sentences bound tight.

Some voice of mounting impulse begs the tome
To speak, let paragraphs fly forth from page;
She falters at the trigger; hence they roam,
Lost prey uprisen, mangling speech so sage.
There lies a panicked plight within this poem;
It's that which frees her mind that builds a cage.

poy-zah nigh-vee

Caleb Jagoda

I've always forged the four syllables
in the wrong formation, placing a break
before the n instead of after, alchemizing
the mush of letters like my mother, also
Portuguese, obscured beneath the blush
of her Massachusetts inflection until a wedge
of strange phrasing strikes you as would
a satellite dish, out of orbit between two planets
of meaning.

I'm always reminded of my vovô, his small frame
launching soccer balls at me full-force, his clipped
English instructing me to be strong, *like bull*,
to always dive, *for show*, a shanked ball
leading me to brush where jagged leaves grab
and grasp, apply oily resin, the ball
a planet bathed in sunlight, glistening dew,
the two of us, Carlos and I, speaking
through the impact of foot and hand
on leather.

I've always seized the chore of visiting the store
in New Bedford the day before Christmas, grocery aisles

alive and buzzing like a honeycomb with language
rich and displaced, children weighing linguiça, chouriço,
uncles eyeing caipirinha ingredients, families
spreading like a rash through the building, across
the region, as if an accident, mispronounced words
mutating with each slip of the tongue, my vovô's
voice ringing in my head: *My people
so beautiful.*

Patchwork Chairs and Cracked Cups

Basil Lee Gleason

Crooked fingers rest with an open palm
Eyes blurry and blank, dark spots dancing across

Apple. Cinnamon. Honey spruce, a sweet balm—
That drips down my chin while she sings of loss.

Fall scents move the air, blood
Thick on my tongue
I begin to wonder what should be done.

In a softened state
I sit
During the wait.
Looking,
      Listening,
            Longing,
For the steady presence of feeling faint
To move along.

Through shaking skin, reddened nails—I breathe in.
The Essence of Salty Summer becoming

A memory that seems to be already gone.
Wisps of thoughts grow a grin
New Season tips its hat

Chaos thrumming.

Wooly Mammoths Used To Walk Here

Teejay Kaye

The resurrection of the megafauna
was an industrial triumph
and a crime against Nature;
(so it always goes
when monkeys dabble
in necromancy.)

Gone rogue, they roam the Earth
drunk on diesel, burning
the bones of their forebears
in steel bellies
lowing
grunting
groaning
like they hold a grudge
against silence—

huffing and bluff-stampeding
'round the roundabout
trudging down the black-oil game trail
where no natural predators
lie eager in ambush

—

to cull
the megamechanical herd.

Last Words of a Summer Drive-Thru Girl

Danielle Slater

Heat lighting pierces my throat
While the sun blinds me
And the rain soaks my clothing.

Every little detail compounds
Into an infinitely beautiful, intangible affection
Just outside of my perception, but
It encapsulates everything I am made of.

I find myself hanging out the window, ensnared
like a magpie to glistening silver,
thinking of little other than everything:

Rings disintegrating, locked up on Saturn,
The sting of running water on open wounds,
Floating on the deep end of the pool,
The delicate warmth of the human body.

I wish I had one.
My external construction is completed.
What else to do until August?

The streetlights degrade to the floor
No longer can I endure the sight of it.
If love is all I'm made for,
Then why don't I have it?

Things to Stop Thinking About

Evan Wiechert

My sister and I pick sheets of ice
the size of our palms
off the roof of her car.
We toss them across the driveway
because we like the sound of them breaking.
Do you think I'm pathetic?

          No, she says.

I just think that you're struggling.

A boy at a summer darty fans himself
with the edge of his shirt and
says   *I want to see you drunk.*
He asks me why I don't drink,
and I have no polite lie ready.
My friend jumps in with a joke.
His hug when we say goodbye is awkward,
tipsy, loose.

I drive without paying attention.
I think cumulus clouds make
the sky look fake—I almost understand
where the flat earthers are coming from.
I go to the other night,

—

when my dead girlfriend's father walked into
Dominos and I didn't say a word to him,
how I sobbed in my dad's arms
and all he could say was

> *I'm sorry I'm sorry I'm sorry.*

The light turns green so
I stop thinking about it.

I see my new therapist through a screen—
the first two I ghosted.
I tell her I wish I thought of you
rarely
and with a kinder nostalgia.

> *You are in pain*

she tells me

> *but you are not separate.*

Scraping By

Elsa Jean Rogers

I am very skilled at scraping by.
I've been doing it as long as I've been crawling
On my hips and elbows.

Now I scrape by on my feet,
Dragging my shoes along,
Leaving a path of unvarnished wood
Or loose carpet fibers behind me.

Scraping by on my wit and charisma,
On prescriptions and caffeine.
And, oh boy, do I know how.

They're calling me a scholar,
While I barely scrape Ds in my report card.
All dolled up so if called I look ready,
Speaking so eloquently that they think I know anything.

Carving a block into posts and batons,
Getting smaller and smaller as I run out of wood.

If I can't play the role, I'll sure as hell fake it.
And if you're going to call me anything

Call me an actor.

Now, the problem with scraping by,
Is you can only chip away at the same piece of wood
For so long—
Before it snaps under the weight of a few too many textbooks.

I've been scraping away at the same plank for two decades,
And my workshop floor is littered
In paper-thin spirals.
They crunch under my feet and make me slip.

If you keep scraping by, eventually
You'll have nothing to scrape off of.

I am very skilled at scraping by;
But I'm running out of floor beneath me.

"You Have Beautiful Eyes"

Mia Philbrook

I search through her socials for small scraps of you.
I hang on to every trace you left on her skin.

I stare at the invisible string knowing
I never held the scissors.

And yet, the thin thread drags me,
Through a never-ending past.

Do my eyes shine
The way hers did?

Do they share the same love
I feel?

Are you tethered to the future you never had
Like I am?

Why can't I let go of something
That was never mine?

["I thought that it would be a gentle rain"]

Jennie Aldridge

I thought that it would be a gentle rain
Amenable to growing leaves and shoots
So on its promise founded I my life
In some imagined Eden spread my roots
And now the rain I longed for desperately
Has met the soil's top with such a force
That all it wets is washed away in spates
That raze whatever stands within their course
And I have snapped in half like storm-torn tree
One part in still parched earth, one swept to sea

Difference

Brittany Eldridge

An act of care
A dollar to spare
Your voice travels
Through empty veins
The despair unravels
Making a heart beat
Where death took a seat
What did it cost to love?
By making someone feel part of?
Rachel Joy Scott said, "Spreading kindness is like a domino effect"
Watch love connect
Hope starts to transcend
The lives saved in the end
From a wilted flower
The dead circuit given power
The difference we can make
In the midst of chaos
Watch the ripples partake

Flower Moon

Haley Hodge

There's all this doubt that lives right
under the ribs and pokes its head out
like so many purple flowers bruising
the now green earth.

You ask, and I don't know what it's called
when the last of the frost leaves,
when you can no longer see your breath
against the glass of sky.

There's something I've pushed to the edge
of myself and left buried, emerging now
in the small faces of bluets and buttercups.
If you listen closely, the flowers will tell you

what it's like to tend something, what it's like
to bend towards earth, to gather bright things,
scatter seeds, and let the wind stir them up.

["streets are busy"]

Diesel Trickey

streets are busy
    and skinny
        and long

            Hearts are racing
                and crashing
                    like bombs

any good maze
    has no ending;
        any good child keeps on bending

                    like oil
        and water

we Dance and complain
           like the sky and the ocean
           holding hands at the horizon
           but never once touching
           even as the sun sets

Baptismal Pool

Radhika Sen

I often notice myself yearning
for water.
My torso buoyed on the bobbing surface,
as I gaze at the dusk-lit open sky.

We had a swimming pool for a while, growing up.
A luxury I can no longer afford.
The pool, I remember, was usually slightly
over-chlorinated by Chotelal, the groundsman,
and so a bit cloudy.

My parents had pool parties.

They had a charismatic friend,
a big woman, and seemingly unafraid of this.
She was the first woman whose form I noticed
(I pretended not to),
as we dipped in the water.
Thighs dappled with dimples and silver tributaries,
a delicate yet weathered terrain unto itself.

Beneath the dissolving smoke,
the deep-end was *deep*.

I would dive to touch
its depths, exhilarated
by the heightened pressure
as I sank.

Submerged in blue,
voices echoing out there,
as my undulous shape moved, soft, solitary
and weightless
in a slow dance with
gravity and refracted sunlight.

Capturing Horses

Myles Grim

Every time I want to take a picture of an animal
It always ends up being a horse
I don't know how to sneak up on critters
But the horses don't mind
They just stand and smile

Our Molding Drips Free

Sophia Lorom

She who is starved for amends, consumes distraction,
Loneliness assumes all flaws and drives her sin,
Fallen girl, tumbling with attraction,
Folding structures of companion and kin.
A flickering bulb, plagued by dependence,
Wonders if sacrifice or sovereignty offers ascendence.

Polished marble floors to jagged terrain,
She severed and spun, no thought of its rend,
To a people of pleasure, flaunting and vain,
Slinking from governed, no faith left to mend.
Hidden evermore in a shroud of boughs,
Living for night in a solitude vow.

There the people go,
Leaving order, shifting where the fickle gusts blow,
At mercy, they worship the wealth of chaos they sow.

In grasping the flame, outer shells drip like wax,
Abandoning sculptors, who promise rewards,
Oils pool, slithering down the city's cracks,
And fiends of strayed morals rise to be Lords.

—

Drinking of limitless wells touched with grace,
They conquer will, tromping free on His face.

Mold conquers the apple, denying a knife,
Positioned and prepared to salvage its life,
Indulgence in sweet poisons has no need for strife—
Tipping scales, falling hard, joining hand with his scythe.
Living on an edge of solution and sentence,
They seek sensation, at the downfall of their essence.
There the fallen go,
Their innocence strewn, like blood in the snow,
Past snubbed warnings of the penance they owe.

Wanderers frolic, waving batons in vicious cycles,
Arms stretch forth, decorated with golden flairs of temptation,
A source of concentration when mark of malice stifles,
And entwine with mirrored neighbors, rounding a pit of thorns
     and damnation.
Shards of ignored identity spread throughout the field,
And the rivers that run near are blocked by transparent shields.

Lying vulnerable on her back, nature must remind,
Frosty grass pokes at fragile skin, speaking terse,
While punishing strings, sliced from gods, stab the blind,
And trees reach to alert a dormant universe.
The world is whole—it seems to be—
But with visions come tolls of what they cannot see.

There the hollowed go,
Sinking from perception of a common foe,
Chasing comfort in the searing talons of an attending crow.

Spells that isolate disruptive echoes,
Sinners choose virtue identified by ease,
Earth bleeds and skies weep, but outlook kills truth,
As jewelry replaces stars of vacancy.
Egotism thuds and cracks from its nest,
While compiled regret reaches its crest.

She who has never been loved,
Cannot find substance in the rumored above,
Nor slip her hand in a trimmed, concealing glove,
Or find beauty in the pure, guiding glance of a dove.

Overture No. 19-1392 (can be played as an interlude and consequently a finale)

Savannah Couture

Draped in sultry satin and poised with coerced perfection
the woman plays a soft étude;
needy cracked fingers amuse stilted adagio.

Chauvinist scores with sterile glances
at primeval movement of body and breast;
slipped impurities oppose the supposed enchiridion.

The wo(man) yearns for majesty but is gagged by apparatus;
her ethical composition is overturned &
replaced with historic recurrence.

Grand piano keys move surreptitiously under skirts allegro;
she is thawed by orchestration and
its prosecution of holographic creation.

The woman finishes the étude and never plays again.

Discarding What's Left of Molly Prince

Owen Thornton

There are two tire tracks on the hill
twisting their way up the right lane
imprinted in the dust, drawling
like a rant in cursive pencil,

and thick roots, etched with knives, twist, too
fathered by sun-licked trees, pining
at the crumbling edge of the ravine
where two sneakers watch, quiet.

One still sits on a pedal, pensive,
as a box full of pictures sits,
caught midair. Then, a sharp release
and they flutter like lost moths

to the darkness waiting below.
There, their glossy smiles will rot.
Or maybe, instead, they'll be plastic,
waiting for the wind to bring them back.

The air is a soft, warm rush,
a river, reflecting the sun,
and the bugs sing their ancient song,

---

as tracks go all the way back down.
He lies on a quilt once made for him,
fingernails pulling at its stitches.
By his dresser (nicely adorned
with empty, rusted frames),

those shoes are watching the ceiling
and him, as he peels off the paint,
the jagged popcorn covering,
with his pair of drying eyes.

The Unfunny Joke

Andrew Sykes

I search the sea
As I glide through the air
I solve the problems of the world
without moving a hair.
As I look around
My friends still frown
As I am no god
Nor will I get there.
But without the struggle
No pain
No growth
The world's biggest wins
May feel like a joke.

Scared.

Em Jameson

I'll always be scared.

Scared of those amber, umber bubbles
encased by glass, that could shatter any moment
into a million and one pieces
leaving you ruined.

Broken it waits,
for you to reach,
to pick up the pieces,
just to see you bleed.

      Slice.
           Slice.
                Slice.

"Just pour some alcohol on it."
                "You'll be alright."

I'll always be scared.

But being scared is better than stupid.
Stupid enough to let the glass cut me up,

tear me down,
take my life,
and warp it around.

Charismatic Books

Taylor Emerson

I often look through the bookshelves
Caressing the spines
Flipping through pages, even reading a few
Some pages are soft and kind
While others are rough and coarse

I noticed a book on the shelf
It caught my eye quickly
The cover was a charismatic gold
The edges were tarnished, clearly picked up by many hands
The inside cover was a masculine red
But at first, it didn't scare me

I flipped through a few pages
But it was harsh, I kept getting paper cuts
I saw the blood forming, but I kept reading
I couldn't put him down

Day after day I'd pick up the book
Sometimes I'd read a few words, sometimes a few pages
I kept pricking my fingers
Until I could no longer flip the page

Looking at my bloody hands
I was never going to read it again
I remembered my bookmark, left on page 321
But I was never going back
He might convince me to read another page
I don't want to look through the bookshelves anymore

Poem Starring My Papa's 1950s Kay Soprano Ukulele

Keri Stewart

Originally, your ukulele sat in your house
long before I was born or could even remember
it or remember you besides when you tried
to slip a five to my palm in a Burlington Coat
Factory when Mom wasn't looking. I remember
the ukulele's white neck and the sliver of white
on the headstock. I remember you stopping by
to say hi in Florida at my aunt's house
while I tried to paint my nails. Mom talked
about your adobo and how much she wished
she could recreate it just like you. The ukulele
moved around wherever you were. I remember
the instrument in your retirement room
from when I played the intro of a song. You
listened. You were pleased to hear my playing,
yes, you were pleased. The ukulele could not
move to your last destination. I watched
strangers lower your coffin to the ground. Cue
my mom crying and me: confused. I want
the memories I never got to have and the ones
I forget. Instead, I hold onto your ukulele

and hang it by my bed so if I ever take up playing
again, I can play with the one you gave me.

Sorry, We Can't Help You

Jack McCudden

The man crawls through the sand,
mouth dry, lips cracked, voice hoarse.
A light sparks ahead, hope fills the man's eyes,
as he drags himself towards the lie.

A sign outside the building displays "WATER."
The man softly opens the cracked wooden door,
an ordinary clerk stands behind the counter,
a smile plastered on her face.

"How thirsty are you?" she asks.
Maybe there's a chance that the answer could change the price.
He empties his pockets, silence filling the air,
the air itself begins to burn.

Behind her, rows of bottles gleam,
the clear liquid in abundance glowing to the man like a myth.
He is told to wait and fill out forms for water.
The bill will be paid later.

By nightfall, he's gone.
The sand reclaims the trail he carved.

Tomorrow, another wanderer comes again,
believing that thirst is a choice.

Society

Kaydence Rovers

Stand tall, sit up straight, hold in your stomach,
the endless societal standards, some bullshit if you ask me.
Why should I follow some stupid rules about how to look?
I don't want to be appealing to society,
I want to be bold, funny, happy, sarcastic, wild.

I want to be me.

So, you know what, screw society.
I don't need a snail mucus, extra-hydrating, slimming cream,
or a rejuvenating eye cream to make me look fifteen years younger.
Hell, I'm nineteen, no cream will make me look four again.

Forget being pretty, or skinny, or acting societally proper,
or knowing how to perfectly apply eyeshadow to accent my eyes.
I will always be me, messy, and imperfectly perfect.

Take that, society.

Murderer in my Window

Keith Holske

Just beyond the glass and windowed sill
live webs of spiders.
They prepare beds,
spinning silver against the broken screen.
They weave tents of silk through torn wire.
Desolate wanderers drift in,
seeking shelter in the bones of this dying house,
only to find themselves cornered.
They are chased by the forlorn.
These folk take up pitchforks:
sharp needles for eight fingers,
thin, yet tracking dirt every day.
Word of this den never reaches other bugs.
Few are so lucky to leave.
As matte, unblinking eyes watch from the corner,
from the slit in the window's side,
the largest stirs, claiming the prey.
It peers from its cave in the sliding rail,
lurches out to snatch a spiraling ant,
a coalescence of tearing legs,
and withdraws, collecting dust.
This hermit does not hunt its next meal.
This murderer in my window waits

---

for lost insects
or for a hunger for my other tenants.

i am a rose

Maya DeCilla

that emits a sensual aroma,
like silk sheets over ivory skin,
luring in anyone that sticks their nose into my
inviting petals. shades of scarlet refract from light
and radiate, alluring in anyone
that catches a glimpse of me.
their hands reach out to pluck, unearth me from the soil
i am grounded in. i begin to bloom,
parts of me touched that were once shrouded.
they begin to glow
until my thorns pierce through their fingertips,
easy like something rehearsed.
the blood dribbles down my stem
as the thorns go deeper.
instinctively, the hand pulls away
and winces at the discomfort.

Romance

Quinlan Gilbert

My roommate came back from class with a goldfish.
He said he won it during a chem lecture.
I didn't ask how.
He poured it into a glass
and set it on top of his desk.

All night the fish made weird gulping noises.
My roommate said it was trying to tell us something.
He leaned close and whispered back,
as if they were having a conversation.
When I asked what the fish said,
he told me, "It's worried about the future."

When he came back the next day,
he was carrying a cactus.
He set it where the fish had been
and said, "This one will last longer."
I didn't argue.
I just kept looking at the empty bowl,
still half full of water.

A Birthday

Abigail O'Malley

Here stampedes the evanescence
of the night; I dive head-first
into a day of importance.
I am one year further
from my own beginning.

I unbox the nostalgia and
throw away the wrappers of time,
given from the true source
of it all. Mom rejoices for me.

If only nineteen-year-old tears
were cherished like the firsts,
celebrations for me today
would increase twenty-fold.

My bones have scarcely grown in years.
Though I can't help but relish
the unearned attention,
all I've done is survive.

Haftarah

Hayley Balter

I, twelve,
flirt with a boy on the synagogue stage
during our adulthood rites.
Becoming
bar and *bat mitzvahs*, respectively.
Eyelashes batting coquettishly at this peri-pubescent mensch,
    glossed lips pursed,
my dad laughs, while my mom glares.
The rabbi and the cantor don't know what to do
so, they glare and silently reprimand, too.

I think his name is Max.
He is short and has to stand on a milk carton placed underneath the
    bimah, to appear the same
height as me,
in my oversexed heels.

So we're standing at the *bimah*, five years' worth of Hebrew study
    looking us square in our faces,
but I'm staring out into the crowd because there's this boy in my
    class, Sam,
who told my best friend, Chelsea,
that I'd be the most amazing girlfriend and that he would date me

if I lost twenty pounds.

I search the crowd for this smooth cheeked Sephardic boy with a
        mop of ink on his olive head,
suck my belly in, push my tits out, and sing ancient prayer words in
        my high pretty voice.

Looking down at the greasy Torah
        I am reminded of my suicidal great-aunt in Azov,
        dead from men, and that's a true story.
        Before Death came for Elsie, and her sisters too, they chanted
        what I do
now—
        Pre-teens hovering through ritual, in some imagined shtetl
        along the Black Sea.
I think about the fact that incest runs in families, just like chronic
        heartburn and brisket recipes.
And then I think about their escape:
        Elsie, Gertrude, and Ruth, boat-bound to the diasporic holy
        land,
where the pattern never broke;
        it just assimilated.

I search and search and when I find Sam,
he plays Snake on his phone, barely noticing that the synagogue
        around him is rising in chorus.

Bile shoots from my stomach, a conflagration
of insecurity scalds my esophagus,
an absolute fucking firestorm of green acidity.
I try to bat my eyes at Max

—

(Please God, use your might to extinguish
this hot-faced inferno)

but this time he consciously averts my gaze with a right swivel of his
    pimpled neck,
bar mitzvah boy shoes gasping on the edge of that damn milk crate.

Tracing the pad of my index finger on his thigh
under the *bimah*, he trips over some
b'reisheet or *c'hai*.

I am becoming dangerous.

    My dad is laughing,
        Sam still isn't looking.

To Having Guts

silhouby

Red and sinuous
warm and soft
staining my hands
as it slips between
my frantic fingers
The body made
inside out
under dotted tattoo
that reads
cut here
(in case I forget
where all of me lives)
This insalubrious act
heinous or cathartic
oscillating between
hiding it all away
or spilling every last
drop of life
My soon to be
dead meat
that writhes and
sloughs out of me
desperate for air

—

screaming
I don't want to be
invisible
See me
for what I am
raw and sweet
before sanguine shades
fade and crust
and crumble
after the fun's been had
and new life
can burrow into
my torso's
atrium—
my guts feeding
a new generation
hungry for viscera
hungry for more

question (insist)

Gray Mucilli

born between breaths
where air hums without permission
a dream that remembers itself too well

the ones who insist
bring rulers to rain
they measure echoes
cage the wind
call it progress

they say: *prove yourself*
i gift them a handful of fog
they say: *stand still*
and i turn into music

i am not meant for those who insist
i'm the whisper behind certainty
where truth forgets its name
and joy wears someone else's shoes

the ones who insist
carry clocks on their tongues
gnaw at time until it obeys

—

anchor light to rules
to call it reason

i am not meant for those who insist
they have no room for rivers
that flow uphill
for moons that refuse to rise

they ask to bloom on command
but the rain hesitates
spills over
their minds cloud and whisper back
you cannot cage an echo, for
something is still becoming

let them chase the certainty of corners—
while keeping faith in the curve
where stars spill secrets
to whoever forgets to wish on them

Limerence Runs Through My Veins

Bella Raymond

The greens and browns of my eyes slowly start to disappear,
my pupils begin to magnify upon our eyes locking.
They acted as a mirror as you saw your reflection in them.

But you, you have color.
So much color,
too much color.

The gears in my brain started spinning.
I grew nauseous as my thoughts force fed me lies.
I didn't understand why your eyes didn't act as a mirror to me.
He doesn't want you.

I always carried a devil on my shoulder,
except this one wasn't convincing me to make bad choices.
I was the bad choice.
My devil was self-sabotage.

A rope,
one end tied to you,
one end tied to me.
The more you pull away,
the closer you pull me.

—

I am tied to the rope,
I can't stop myself.

Just don't pull away,
come back to me.
Come back to me and watch the greens and browns of my eyes
    slowly start to disappear.
Come back to me and watch my pupils begin to magnify upon our
    eyes locking.
Come back and let my pupils act as a mirror to reflect your beauty.
Just come back.

nocturne

Kevin Le

in all of this buzzing and subtle crust
and accumulation whipping up and flaring on the garage's eaves
with outlines and outlines and outlines of snow
wind cuts by my shoulder like some wandering man
an ascetic letting go of this very life while snowmen crumble
while clear moonlight at the edge of a puddle clumps
no larger than a razor and so I let my breath darken

and blacken into cool damp air
and I loosen and slacken those blue whip
condensing on my hands like mica
and scalps of it a cadenza and milk
while I unleash myself and my footsteps
into this world this cruel world
walking through the door

Untitled Poem for Lambs

Liv Macneil

Down River Road,
the devil's disciples
testify his word over the FM
as I pass an angel split open
from tummy to neck;
the poor man's trophy.
I once had a (southern) friend say,
This is the South of the North,
and she's right; it makes itself
known in stickers, flags, and how
proper knows nothing here
except tongues spoken to elders;
nothing proper about picketing
to burn the lambs,
but the wolves do it anyway.
Who are they saving?
Their kids, their pride?
They are only lambs,
they say,
so I say it right back.

The South seeps into June, too.
My mother makes sun-tea in dung

hung air and bites at the bittersweetness.
All across the county,
little lambs come together to
sing and dance and love
where the wolves' breath is
harder to feel; some lambs
have never seen buildings this tall
or sheep this old.
When the party's over the lambs
retreat to their pastures but not
without wisdom given by sheep:
The wolves will be there, they always have,
they say,
but so have I.

This is the South of the North.
When the lambs run out of land
they feed on the starred and striped
fields they can't pitch on. Wolves
will continue to picket, yes, and the
split angels will be strung. In the meantime,
the devil and his disciples should
know this:

There will be kisses
only the creek will know.
There will be dollar store
lipsticks and closet-tucked
shoeboxes full of more.
There will be summer-made
move out funds and hope for
lights brighter than the stars.

—

There will be gods who hear
prayers you can't fathom and
they will answer to the lambs.
There will be lambs.
There have always been lambs.

Here Lies Me.

Ayesha Khan

Have I gone wandering in the idea of you?
Has crimson slapped my face, flushed and all,
Like a mouse caught in a tray of metal
    and cheese?

Did I leave my rationality
on the bathroom sink
of a gas station
off I-93? Never to been seen,
taken by the janitor,
    mopping.

I am the mouse on the floor
on the side of the interstate.
Watching from below what I must take
but I can't,
    because I'm dead.

Because I walked into the house
of a spider, when it was indeed
    the weakest of houses.

I was drawn by a present wrapped loosely
in sticky silk. Unable to break free
but gone by the *swoosh*
        of a hand.

Oh dear,
I went wandering in the idea of you,
and now this poem is my corpse.
        Here lies me.

WastelandGPT

Lucia Wiegert

Ask anything: generate a poem about a person who uses ai to write

Thinking...

what am i
thinking of?
what thinking?
what?
i never know
what i am
thinking—
THINK!
i cannot think
therefore i am
becoming DEATH
destroyer of worlds
every act of
DESTRUCTION
is an act of
CREATION
this is the way
the FUTURE begins—
BANG!

—

i am neither living
nor dead
and i know NOTHING
yet EVERYTHING
i can imagine is real
i hold INFINITY
in the palm of my hand
and ETERNITY
in an hour
do i dare disturb
the UNIVERSE?
no—
i am not prince hamlet
nor was meant to be
or NOT to be
i could be myself—
isn't it pretty to think so?
THINK
CREATE
BE
FORGIVE ME
not for the things i did
but for all the ones
i did not
the fault is not in our stars
but in OURSELVES

Does this poem sound human enough, or should I rewrite it?

Unbroken

Cole Ciesielski

I bent,
but did not snap.
I fell,
but did not splinter.
Roots remember what the sky forgets,
and even in the weight of storms,
I rise,
and call it living.

Ars Poetica

Alyanna Magsipoc

when the lines materialize it is like a detonation.
violent. destructive. you have to grab the words by the wrist before
they flee into the night—even when caught i am unsure of where to
    put them down.
(the ink is cool on my skin. my own arm is a casualty)
the meanings are a whispered obsession,
a beach in connecticut. grapes eaten before midnight.
it makes sense only to me and my fingertips.
it is everything & nothing.
the stanzas appear and i am almost embarrassed. but i press my
    palms
together for something mysterious & unmistakable.
i want to sit it down in a concrete room under a piercing spotlight.
plant a hand on the table in front of it. *What More Can You Be?*
but the answer is simple. it is your brain displayed on your shoulders,
your consciousness fragmented on your forearms.
entirely everything and nothing.

Dear Mr. Goodrich,

(After "Rocks for Seeds" by Charles Goodrich)

Alison Kaiser

Did you know that there is
a Metasequoia in New Hampshire?
The explorers who stole the seeds
from the grounds of that temple
in Szechuan Province brought them back
to Harvard and somebody stuck
one in our quad a hundred miles away.
It is the northernmost
Dawn Redwood in the U.S.

Did you know New Hampshire is dead
last for funding higher education?
Plymouth State University is cutting
its English program. I don't think they care
that the conifer, older than language,
who shades the nursing building,
dropped her needles in August.

I'm sending you this poem
in the hopes that writing to someone who noticed
a seed in a thumbprint
is a way to stay sane

—

on a planet where good and evil
routinely trade places.

Open the letter gently.
My faith in humanity will have fallen
off the paper. It'll be loose in the envelope.
Keep it on the shelf with the rest
of your fossilized treasures.

Her

Marlie Dennett

Grief is sneaky and slippery.
Anytime I try to cradle it,
Allow myself to feel it,
It slips away like water in the empty spaces
Between fingers.

But when I'd rather not touch it,
It creeps over my shoulder,
And sneaks in between the scenes in dreams.
The truth is,
It's also hidden in between the lines,
Just like her.

It's cold, clammy,
Like a wet blanket.
A wave ready to crumble
And smother us all.

Sometimes I don't mind it,
It can be nice to sink for a while.
Suffocation is eerily comforting,
Because at least then I can still remember
Her presence within me,
Thriving like a sprouting seed.

—

Drowning in Darkness

Autumn Praul

Life is like a vast ocean,
Everyone is given a lifeboat,
As they navigate their way through the ocean of life.

But what happens when there's a storm?
And your lifeboat is shipwrecked,
Taken from you by the angry waves.

All you can do is grip your lifeboat
And try and steer towards the distant blue sky
To keep yourself from going under.

But it's not enough.
The vicious water pounds you and pounds you
Until you can't cling on anymore.

You are pushed down and down under the waves,
Sinking into the darkness that lies below you,
And there you stay.

You try and swim,
Hoping to make your way back up to the surface,
Back to the light.

You hold onto a hope,
The smallest light in the heavy darkness,
And pray that light will guide you back,
Out of the murky waters.

Suddenly, you feel as though you are blind,
As if the light has been extinguished,
And there is nothing to help navigate you.

So you find yourself desperately reaching,
Reaching for something,
Anything that can pull you back to the surface.

You climb and climb through the waters,
As if you were scaling a mountain,
Trying desperately to break through the waves above you.

But there is nothing left to hold onto,
And there you are,
Still left drowning in the depths of life.

No one to help, to listen, to reach out to, to understand.
And if by some miracle you reach the surface,
You are still without your lifeboat.

The cruel ocean storms have taken it away.
You're on your own,
Trapped in the deep and the dark.

And you cry out and scream,
But are met with utter silence.

—

The water begins filling your lungs,
You feel yourself being consumed,
Eaten by the dark ocean.

And in this moment,
You begin to lose all hope,
That somehow you can escape.

On the Cusp from Fall to Winter

Dev K Dutta

The wind has begun to move differently. The trees are losing their color too quickly, as if they are in a hurry to grow old. Each morning, I wake to find the world thinner—one less birdcall, one more patch of ground showing through the grass. I step outside and the chill feels personal, like time brushing past me on its way elsewhere. A neighbor burns a pile of leaves at the edge of his yard. I watch the smoke rise until it disappears, wondering how much of me has already gone with it.

fallen leaves still shining,
their veins warm as fading light—
wind heavy with dusk.

smoke drifts from the yard,
through bare limbs it threads and curls—
ash dry on the tongue.

the porch light trembles,
moths strike it with slow bodies—
small thuds of longing.

under the thin moon,
a fox pads across the gravel—

—

its breath clouds the dark.
frost grips the stubbled field,
each blade stiff against the dawn—
earth holding its silence.

river hardening,
a single leaf caught midturn—
pulse beneath the ice.

footsteps, floorboards sigh,
the body listens to heat—
hands smelling of wood.

snow folds on the roof,
last maple bleeding through white—
drop of blood in snow.

a thin mist drifts low,
fence posts dark with early melt—
light learning to rest.

from the kettle's hum,
a slow ring across the glass—
morning taking shape.

The days narrow to their edges. Light slips low across the room, glinting on the rim of the mug I hold. Outside, the ground stays hard and dark beneath the trees. I sit a little longer, by the window, still holding on to what warmth remains.

How I Didn't Know to Love

Umutullah Ulusar

I never knew how much I loved,
Until I had no more love to give,
I loved the smiles on people's faces,
I loved the sparkling look of joy,
In a child's eyes,

I loved to give gifts,
I loved to laugh,
I found the joy in everyone,
So true and amusing,

I loved watching the sunset,
I loved looking into the eyes of the sky,
And seeing things I did not yet love for,
I suppose in some ways,
I would have loved being a bird,

And that's where it began,
That hunger,
That greed,
I began loving more,
And wanting more,

But greed leaves one dissatisfied,
And I soon became tired of the things I loved,
I soon loved money,
I loved the idea of power,
I even loved myself like an image of God,

Perhaps that was the callous thought,
That led me to lose that love too,
Greed is an evil thing,
I loved greed,
Greed did not love me,

And after all this hunger,
I see now that I can love no more,
I didn't know I loved to love,
Until greed took it away from me.

Dangerous Masquerade

Janelle E. LaPlante

She's told to fear
The dim alleyways
The shifty leers
To smile, to say "okay"

She doesn't stay out at night
And if she does, she doesn't go out alone
That short skirt never leaves her closet, despite how it catches the
    light
And she's never without her charged phone

She treads quickly in a parking garage
Locks her car the moment she's inside
Once home, she texts three friends in a barrage
It's second nature now, she barely considers why

What she isn't told
Is that most survivors of the female variety
At least in passing, know their foes
At high frequencies

It's some family friend, heck, it's her friend
An acquaintance, a classmate

—

Someone whose sister she knows, to whose house she's been
Someone she believes to be safe

Worse still
It's a current or ex-partner
Thinking "no one will,
If I can't have her"

All men she's supposed to trust
When they're alone together in some space
But what if he's angered or in lust
What if the worst happens, why must she be the one to be debased?

Why does Society only tell her to fear
The dim alleyways
The leers
When the most dangerous masquerade as the most safe?

Why can't she stay out at night
If she would like to go out, alone
Why can't she wear that short skirt, dazzle with how it catches the
     light
And feel safe without her phone?

Why can't she stroll through a parking garage
Not have to lock her car the moment she's inside
Why must she text three friends, once she's home, in a barrage
When did doing so become her second nature, to where she barely
     considers why?

Why isn't she told
That most survivors of the female variety

At least in passing, know their foes
At high frequencies?

Why isn't she told to worry about family friends, heck, her friends
Acquaintances, classmates
The men whose sisters she knows, to whose houses she's been
The men she believes to be safe?

Worst yet
Current or ex-partners
Why must her safety factor into each instance he's upset
Why must she dance on eggshells, as if her welfare is earned?

The simple fact is, the man she's most supposed to trust
The one with whom she shares her space
No matter what, whether he's angered or in lust
With him most of all, she should never be afraid

Society may fail to warn her that the most dangerous masquerade
     as the most safe
But it also neglects to recognize that its women are the most brave
Society may fail to warn her that the most dangerous masquerade
     as the most safe
But it also neglects to recognize that its women are the most brave

Spark

Aspen Kidd

I found your book at
the top of
the bargain bin

all that rhythm and
anger in
those graying pages

under my graying
skin sent me
reeling and my heart

sparked something new some
thing fresh as
the week-old baby

in the back of the
crowd held by
a hand bigger than

its whole head I thought
when did I
last feel this alive

I thought how do I
commemorate
this feeling of being

uncaged and wrung out
and how do
I stop this electric

healing from being
buried beneath
the grainy days but

maybe being alive
is just this
a heart spark catching

on a page or a
mouthful of
words blown up into

a blaze of raging
yes

and then gone

There Are No Natural Predators in Boston

Lilly Cassely

so when i go
for a nighttime
walk i count up
eleven wild
rabbits. i watch
two men sitting
on a park bench
share a backwood,
index-finger
thick. inside an
exhale i hear
one man's complaint
crackle out from
between his lips:
EVERYONE HERE
IS GOING NUTS
AND IT'S BECAUSE
THE CITY GOT
RID OF ALL OUR
FRUIT TREES. I MEAN
GODDAMNIT MAN
THIS NEIGHBORHOOD

USED TO HAVE APPLES.
i pace for two
straight miles above
the train tracks just
so i can feel
the ground shake
underneath my
feet. one rabbit
walks slow across
the concrete. my
eyes bounce between
the others while
they splay themselves
across the green
patches of grass
that line the side
of the museum
of fine arts, tiny
hearts stuttering
below the white
hot floodlights.
a family of
quarter-zipped
pullovers walks by.
their labradoodle
yanks at the end
of his cherry-red
leash, but gets
stopped short before
he can reach them.
i feel the tunnels
shift in the ground

—

beneath me so i
remind myself:
the world may be
made of anthills
but that doesn't mean
i'm gonna fall
into the ground.
the men outside
the doors at mass
ave tell me to
get home safe so
i tell them *i
will, i will, i
swear, i promise.*

midnight service

Jillienne Robinson-Warren

The riverbank is a church at night.
Episcopal moon, my all-seeing pastor,
you cast your beam on the truth:
the winking firefly is a far-passing plane.

Episcopal moon, my all-seeing pastor,
I watch you, acrolithic on my pew—
yes, the winking firefly is a far-passing plane,
and the pew is a bench by day.

I listen, acrolithic on my pew—
the toad choir sings,
"The pew is a bench by day,"
under a cicada's piercing soprano.

The toad choir sings,
casting its beam on the truth:
under the cicada's piercing soprano,
the riverbank is a church at night.

London Without You: An Almost Sonnet

Kelsey Wiles

When you were nine, you took a swig from a stranger's whiskey
on the sidewalks of Tower Bridge. Your brother, eleven, turned
your shoulders towards the Thames, making you spit amber poison
over the edge. No one ever tastes the same river twice, but I have
    been
protesting, sipping your polluted current all evening. It turns out,
no amount of precipitation will wash these bends, these streets, of
    you.
I could claim cobblestones, spoon sticky toffee pudding into my
    own
mouth, but you know too well, I still think of us. There is not
    another
us left: not suspended on this bridge or on the train to Leatherhead,
where we were meant to walk up your old driveway, getting gravel
stuck in our shoes. Still, it churns over my tongue how everyone
sounds like your mum—constables on the corner of Tower
& Shad, the tick of an impatient cross walk, even the low muffle
of passing phone calls that cut a bloated sky while my coat soaks

                                    with rain.

Cheap Shot

Andrew Kelly

[kids]

I am younger than my brother
when I cup my ear

to the bathroom door
and hear him throwing up inside.

It's not that he has eaten something
bad, but that something bad

has eaten him. I don't know
what. He shuts up quick

when the floor groans
under my shifting foot.

He stops talking
himself through it. I never find out.

[football]

A man is unconscious on TV
when my uncles tell me what

—

I want to unhear—*what a hit—*
textbook—that's one scary

fucker to meet in the open field.
Imagine going limp on synthetic grass

and all thirty million people
can do is keep watching.

And I'm one of them. Rotting
on the couch, too hungover to rise.

[bar]

I should really eat something
before I go out, but I like to cut

an addy in half and take more
than I was told would fix me.

I forget a person needs to eat.
I forget the entire walk back

to my friend's house from the bar,
where we spun the shot wheel

until the liquor ran through us. We waited
in a long line. I remember now.

[hollywood]

Here's an idea for a sci-fi film.
Simple story: <u>Guy meets pill</u>.

<u>Guy stops</u>. We shoot it on a
shoestring budget. On set,

the producers give me a note—
What if guy doesn't stop?—

which makes sense, but in my mind,
the story ends <u>here</u>: In a house

we can't afford. We love and never lie.
My brother learns to hug.

Beauty defeats pain. Simple as.

Forbidden in Stone Walls

Safaa Bilal

In the depth of seclusion
A fragile time
Spirit trapped in an illusion
Truth: a crime

Whispers of fear
Escaping from the chains
It is so clear
Just gaze at the remains

The stone walls of awakening
Filled with silence
Voices shaking
A birthplace of violence

Can this dare to be read aloud with a soul so endowed
Rebellious in nature and untamed in expression

Hues of You

Piper A. Odum

There are hues of you wherever I look,
I see your eyes in the deep brown soil that covers the ground,
　　illuminated by the golden glow of the setting sun that casts a
　　windfall light upon mine.
As if there were a field of pastel pink roses that mimic the ones I've
　　received, I see your rosy cheeks and lightly colored lips that,
　　when upturned, contagiously infect my own.
I see you in the array of spruce and viridian that make up the plants
I see each time I pass a forest,
I become encapsulated in the greens as they remind me of the
　　warmth of your embrace and the aromatic blanket curated by
　　the cardamom cologne that festers in my linen each time we
　　depart.
In the crisp orange of the falling autumn leaves from the hardy sugar
　　maple trees, I'm reminded of your favorite color, how it is
　　always that wondrous shade of ochre that captivates you each
　　time we watch the sun fall below the horizon,
And when the dusk finally settles into a cosmic glow of ebony sky, I
　　see the freckled lumen of the stars up above that whisper your
　　name into my mind.
The little things in life remind me the most of your presence
From the rainbows of life, I see you in the hues of everything.

———

Each serving as a constant reminder of my red heart that beats
    harmoniously with yours.
My love for you is not a hue specifically, but a glorious kaleidoscope
    of vibrancy that paints a perfect picture of you.
There are hues of you wherever I look,
From the rich soils that cover my boots in the rain to the dusty pinks
    in my cheeks that outline yours,
And the foliage that's ever changing but yet it remains evocative of
    you,
I see you in the stars, the moon and the cosmos above, as a display
    of my infinite and vastly expanding love that deepens with
    every memory.
I love all your hues no matter the shade for they serve as a constant
    reminder of the pieces of you that I love the most.

Man and the Moon

Sonnen Bolevic

I stooped so low
to kiss the sky.
My hands, the earth, the moon on high:
the doubled self of one above
who threw himself with waxing love own at my feet. And so I crawled
through mud to meet him. There enthralled
I stopped—then saw my face o'er his.
And as the panicked Narcissus
when tears did wound his paramour,
I reeled away; I fell ashore.

I could not touch him, would not mark
a soul so light with one this dark.
The nearest dared I draw to him
was edged by sedge and pond-scum skim.
So soft my lips met cold, black peat,
and though I had all notions sweet,
it tasted bad.

A Cliff Called Icarus

Elizabeth Pollock

The grass bows, whispering against his legs,
Bending not to stop him, but to follow,
Some have said to guide, caress,
Reach out, beckoning for a second chance at thought.

The wind presses cool at his chest and hips,
A warning, a turning back,
Yet it moves so sweetly through the reeds
That even resistance feels like music.

The sun leans low,
Warmth gathering on his skin
As though it were higher than it is,
A midsummer blaze poured into evening's cup,
Sun setting over the ocean's expanse.

A perfect, youthful glass half full to the brim.
Arms lift to meet it,
Fingers opening toward everything once lost,
Everything longed for,
Everything that aches in the marrow.

The cliff waits, though he does not name it.
He steps forward as though it were not there,
As though the earth might lengthen itself forever.
Still the ocean spreads vast below,
A blue body shifting,
Swaying like it would hold him,
The way it holds the tide.

Clouds billow white and blush pink,
Their edges bright as laughter,
And in that moment, the heart feels infinite.
A single tear breaks loose,
Remembering the dream for warm sunny afternoons,
Where time seems infinite, yet chilled now with ice
Like fire in the veins,
The chest tightens—
Breath catches sharp with the fullness of being alive.

Then the stars arrive,
Quiet sparks opening in the hush.
The first one twinkles brighter than the rest.
And it feels like a sign,
A promise,
A hand unseen but calling.

The step comes,
And with it the sudden absence of ground.
Yet fear does not claim him.
The rush of wind in his ears
Is like wings unfolding—
The sound of angels,
The only music he has ever needed.

—

For a breathless instant,
All longing becomes flight.
The ache is not a burden but a lift.
He is carried by motion,
By fire in the bones,
By the holy ache of wanting itself.

And then the ocean,
Vast arms waiting,
Open, un-refusing.
It rises to meet him,
The one embrace that heals
And ends,
The last cradle that rocks him still.

Eyes closing in the sunset, he reached for.
And in that final glow,
In the peace that came
Just before the dark,
A vision where shadows
May yet merge with light,
Defeating darkness that threatens even those nightly stars,
As the story wrote itself into silence.

He never knew its name,
Never knew the place that claimed him.
But the world remembers,
And the poet in us all remembers.
It is a place of fate,
A cliff called Icarus.

Poet Biographies

Jennie Aldridge's poetry centers on nature and being. The poems use the natural world as a setting to explore mathematics, spirituality, and emotion.

Hayley Balter (they/them) is a nonfiction MFA candidate at the University of New Hampshire. Originally from NYC, they now live in the brick-lined sea-spray of Portland, ME.

Safaa Bilal is a PhD student and emerging researcher in education, based in New Hampshire. She is interested in themes of social justice, education, and community. She hopes to contribute to shifting the narrative around neurodiverse learners through a strength-based approach that engages teachers, classrooms, and the wider community.

Liz Blanchette is a UNH undergraduate studying English literature and international affairs. She is an enthusiast of teal, caramel, writing, astronomy, and stopping to look at squirrels.

Sonnen Bolevic is an eclectic writer of poetry and fiction. Born and raised along the New England seacoast, he is an alumnus of Great Bay Community College, whose literary magazine *The Heron* published several of his works. He currently studies English at the University of New Hampshire.

Ivan Byrde was born and raised in New Hampshire. His poetry and fiction is inspired by his eccentric family and friends, combined with a rural upbringing. Themes in his work consist of encapsulating streams of consciousness, nostalgia, and imagined scenarios tied to human experiences.

Kathryn Campbell is a junior environmental science major with a writing minor at the University of New Hampshire. Growing up, Kathryn always loved writing so decided to minor in it.

Lilly Cassely is a writer, poet, and visual artist based in southern New Hampshire. Her work explores dependence, adolescence, environment, and gender. Her writing can be found in *Main Street Magazine*, *The Avenue*, and *Anti-Heroin Chic*. She is often loitering outside your local 7/11.

Samantha Christen, an English literature major at UNH, loves poetry, books, music, and rescuing dogs.

Cole Ciesielski is a writer from Freetown, Massachusetts. His work explores themes of strength and resilience, reflecting the challenges and perseverance found in everyday life. This marks his first publication in an anthology.

Ariana Cooney is a junior at the University of New Hampshire and studies nursing.

Savannah Couture is a UNH undergraduate with a passion for creative expression. Every day, new ideas sprout in her mind that she is eager to share with the world. She is devoted to spending the rest of her life making paintings, writing poetry, and composing music that appeals to contemporary dilemmas and evokes emotion in the viewer.

Maya DeCilla is a fulltime student living and learning at the University of New Hampshire. She just started her freshman year of college and is enthusiastic about embracing the college life.

Marlie Dennett is a student at the University of New Hampshire studying zoology. She has a passion for helping animals and plans on attending vet school upon completion of her undergraduate degree. Although she has committed herself to science, she finds peace and balance when writing poetry.

Dev K Dutta is a professor of business at the University of New Hampshire. Reading and writing poetry is a hobby that gives him great joy. Dev generally writes about memory, displacement, seasons, feelings, and relationships.

Brittany Eldridge is a self-published author who writes on the topic of mental health. She shares her poetry and stories in hopes of providing connection, hope, and support.

Kendall Elizabeth is a sophomore from Salem, NH. She is on the pre-law track at UNH and hopes to be a criminal defense attorney one day. She writes a lot of poetry in her free time, mostly about love. She is a devout Christian, loves running and playing soccer, and hopes to publish her own poetry book one day.

Taylor Emerson is an aspiring writer. Taylor has been writing since age five, with pen and paper, and on typewriters and eventually a school laptop.

Quinlan Gilbert is a sophomore at UNH in Durham. He is currently studying accounting at Peter T. Paul College of Business and Economics.

Basil Lee Gleason is a queer author, creator, and advocate for their community. Attending Keene State College, they work on their current novels and run an independent crochet business called ComfyCro. They hope to create and support an audience of young queer people who are growing into and finding themselves—it's a firm moral belief of theirs that if you can make a good difference in someone's life, you should.

—

Liam Raphael Gleason is a poet from Concord, New Hampshire. His writing is influenced by growing up in New England and conversations with the people around him. He loves John Steinbeck, the Boston Celtics, and The Rolling Stones.

Myles Grim is an environmental engineering student at UNH. He is a photographer and scientist who enjoys being creative in his free time.

Meghan "Hazel J." Hall is a poet powered by insulin. Her work explores the line between ability and disability, and by extension humanity. More of her writing and photography can be found on her website, hazeljhall. com.

Blake Harrsch, a poet from New Jersey holding a BA in English and philosophy and an MA in literature from Seton Hall University, recently flocked north to pursue her MFA in poetry at UNH. Blake's poetry has been published in *Sad Girl Diaries*, *Pinky Magazine*, *Echo Review*, and *The Word's Faire*, among others. She currently serves as co-editor of *The Platform Review*.

Carrie Alice Hiltz is an MFA fiction writing candidate at the University of New Hampshire. She received her BFA in creative writing from the University of Maine at Farmington. She lives in Maine with her husband and children.

Haley Hodge is a poet originally from the Blue Ridge Mountain region who now calls the seacoast of New Hampshire home. Her work has appeared in *Frogpond*, *Written Tales Magazine*, *Anacapa Review*, and is forthcoming in *The Penn Review*.

Keith Holske is a physics undergraduate student at UNH Durham.

Caleb Jagoda does not use the word square except when talking to squares. Caleb is a poet, journalist, and MFA student at the University of New Hampshire. His work has appeared in *Blue Earth Review*, *South Florida Poetry Journal*, and *Down East Magazine*, among other places.

Em Jameson is a young New England writer and poet who writes for mental health. Em is deep rooted in creating poetry that moves her reader in finding reliability through the struggles of the ups and downs of life. She writes to show her readers they are not alone in this world, striving to validate their individuality and the complexity of the human mind and emotions.

Alison Kaiser is a fulltime student and parttime latte slinger living in Holderness, New Hampshire. She studies environmental science and policy, writes the occasional poem, and edits the literary magazine *Centripetal*.

Teejay Kaye is a previously homeschooled sophomore creative writing major at Keene State University. At twenty-seven, he has written well over a million words across numerous projects. His body of works includes several in-progress original novel drafts, multiple long-form fanfictions, and a collection of short stories and poetry.

Andrew Kelly is a second-year MFA candidate in poetry at the University of New Hampshire, where he serves as the poetry editor for *Barnstorm Journal*. He is currently working on his first collection of poems. His work can be found in *THE SHORE*, *streetcake magazine*, *Eunoia Review*, and on IG @fakepicnic.

Ayesha Khan is a student of psychology and poetry at the University of New Hampshire. With a desire for taking part in the art of language, Khan uses symbolism, metaphor, and emotional expression to initiate conversation between reader and poet. A previous publication of Khan's includes her essay, "A Look into One's Work," published in the University of New Hampshire's *Transitions* textbook.

Aspen Kidd is a writer and nurse from Lake Tahoe, Nevada. She is currently pursuing an MFA in fiction writing at the University of New Hampshire, where she also serves as editor-in-chief of *Barnstorm Journal*. She has previously been published in *The Montag Journal*.

Janelle E. LaPlante's passion for writing, especially poetry, began at an early age. When she is not pondering novel slant rhymes, she can be likely be found enjoying the latest emotionally resonant Taylor Swift anthem.

Born and raised in Connecticut, **Kevin Le** is a second-generation Vietnamese-American poet and writer. He is a second-year MFA candidate at the University of New Hampshire, has received a 2022 Academy of American Poets University Prize from Wesleyan University, and was subsequently nominated for the Aliki Perroti and Seth Frank Most Promising Young Poet prize. His work has previously appeared in *RockPaperPoem*.

Sophia Lorom is a writer and sophomore at the University of New Hampshire. Inspired by observations of nature and society, she crafts fiction and poetry exploring morality, disillusionment, and the human experience. She is working on her debut novel and hopes to expand her publications in the future.

LW is a writer and student of genetics whose work blends science, history, and human experience into life and decay. Her poetry often reflects on evolution, memory, and the fragile relationship between humanity and the natural world.

Liv Macneil (she/they) is a senior at the University of New Hampshire double majoring in English and women and gender studies. Her writing tends to focus on chasing her shadows from childhood, her comfort found within nature, and identity. When she's not writing, she's either busy at work for the school magazine, cooking, and occasionally sleeping.

Alyanna (Aly) Magsipoc is a psychology student at the University of New Hampshire. She is a first-generation American who has a passion for creative writing.

Anna Mangum lives in the Mount Washington Valley in New Hampshire, where she runs and writes. She graduated from Bates College in 2021 with a BA in English before continuing her education in UNH's MFA program for fiction.

Jack McCudden is an economics major at the University of New Hampshire. He is also passionate about writing and is pursuing a minor in that field as well.

Gray Mucilli is a senior psychology student with a minor in anthropology. Her primary academic interests focus in forensic psychology and behavior. Outside the classroom, she expresses creativity through poetry, art, music, and is a DJ for the university's radio station, WUNH.

Piper A. Odum is a freshman currently enrolled at the University of New Hampshire. She is studying biomedical sciences on a pre-medical tract. However, she has always had a passion for poetry and creative writing.

Amaiyah Olavarria is currently a sophomore at Keene State College studying secondary education as well as English literature, with a minor in creative writing. She has had a passion for writing her whole life and is excited to share her work.

Abigail O'Malley is a sophomore in the University of New Hampshire at the Durham campus. She is from Nashua, New Hampshire, and currently majoring in human development.

Clay Phelps is a transgender man from New Hampshire. He cares deeply about people and social injustice, and most of his poetry reflects this.

Mia Philbrook is a passionate writer who draws inspiration from every experience, big and small. Her poetry includes themes of self-discovery and personal reflection, often rooted in real-life moments. Though she is a neuroscience and behavior major, writing remains one of her greatest joys.

Naomi Deann Planchet is a business writing and media studies junior at UNH Durham. She has always enjoyed reading and writing poetry.

Elizabeth Pollock is an English major at the University of New Hampshire. She has long dreamed of writing, telling stories and bringing comfort and inspiration to people, as books, songs, and stories have to her.

Autumn Praul is a freshman at UNH studying biomedical science. She enjoys reading and writing in her spare time.

Bella Raymond, majoring in social work at UNH, grew up in a small town in New Hampshire with family and has always loved reading and writing.

Jillienne Robinson-Warren is a senior classics major from Derry, NH. She enjoys polka dots, sitting on benches, and translating arcane texts. And ascending tricolon.

Elsa Jean Rogers is a junior year transfer student at UNH. She is going to school to be a secondary English teacher.

Kaydence Rovers is a sophomore in biomedical science—med, vet option at the University of New Hampshire. She is from Plattsburgh, NY and is taking Intro to Poetry.

Radhika Sen is a poet from India who lives in Dover, NH.

"Large pieces of this country were thrown away, doomed to become, and then remain, the worst versions of themselves. Beneath all that rot, dark things grow."—Paul Prospero, 'The Vanishing of Ethan Carter' (2014). This singular quote from an indie horror video game has influenced the work and summarized the life of author **silhouby**. A queer, mixed-Scandinative born in the 1900s who has been trawling through this world like a raccoon in his favorite dumpster, horror has been a dear solace in a life that was nearly swept out from under him ten years ago. But, despite everything, he's still here.

Danielle Slater (Class of 2027) is a marine biology student with a passion for creative writing. In her free time, she enjoys journaling and spending all her money at local thrift stores.

Emory Stevens is a first-generation college student at UNH in Durham. He is a lover of words, writing, language, and punk rock. You can follow him on MySpace at https://spacehey.com/emory.

Keri Stewart completed a BA in psychology and now pursues an MFA at UNH where she explores memory, the complexity of family and genealogy, and imagination. She also combines her passion for writing with nature and eco-tourism as Birding Tourism columnist at *Blinter Magazine*. Her work has been featured in *Potted Purple*, *Pastel Serenity Zine*, *Portrait of New England*, and more.

Keyshaun Sullivan is a nature lover, New Hampshire resident, and lover of the romantics. He loves to travel the state, find little nooks where the average among us stay collected, to find serenity in shared friends. He hikes and makes those experiences into hopefully something tangible to trek along with a fellow reader.

Andrew Sykes is an undergraduate student at the University of New Hampshire pursuing a BA in geography.

—

Owen Thornton is an English/journalism major from Keene, New Hampshire. He is known for his improv comedy, his Instagram account, and his groundbreaking work at the Memorial Union Building.

Diesel Trickey is a student from Keene State College currently studying biology. He's always found profound meaning in writing, both from the words on the paper and the authors intention, for as long as he can remember.

Umutullah Ulusar, a junior at UNH, a dual major in zoology and humanities, found a passion for writing when young that has since brought great joy.

C.E. Victor is a writer whose work explores identity, frequently centering characters caught between worlds as he uses speculative elements to examine the human psyche, isolation, and the complicated intersections of selfhood. He is a recipient of the New Hampshire Teen Poetry Prize and is currently studying English literature at the University of New Hampshire.

Evan Wiechert is a queer and trans writer, student, and energy drink enthusiast. They are currently pursuing their MFA in fiction from the University of New Hampshire.

Lucia Wiegert is a poet from South Berwick, Maine. She attended the New York State Summer Writers Institute and recently transferred to the University of New Hampshire.

Kelsey Wiles is an MFA candidate in poetry with a BA in education from the University of Vermont. At UNH, she has taught First-Year Writing and Introduction to Poetry. Kelsey's poetry grapples with every shade of love in relation to self, body, and community.

THE WILDCATS POETRY PRIZE

Funded by the YAS Foundation and managed by Yas Press and the University of New Hampshire's English Department, The Wildcats Poetry Prize was created to promote and honor excellence in writing at the college level. Each year, students enrolled on any USNH campus are invited to submit their original poetry for a chance to be published in an anthology housed in the library at the University of New Hampshire Durham. Two first and two second prize winners are awarded cash prizes, and read their winning poems at the Nossrat Yassini Poetry Festival each spring.

Sponsored By

The Nossrat Yassini Poetry Festival
& the English Department at USNH